I0427536

The Step-by-Step Guide to Negotiation and Sales in Any Line of Business

Copyright © 2024 Reginaldo Osnildo

PRESENTATION

It is with great pleasure that I present to you this book: **"The Step-by-Step Guide to Negotiation and Sales in Any Line of Business"**.

Throughout these chapters, you will find powerful techniques and insights to improve your negotiation skills and reach more advantageous agreements in any context.

We'll start by understanding the fundamentals of effective negotiation, then dive into more advanced strategies based on psychology, empathy, asking smart questions, and more. You will learn to deal with challenging situations, such as negotiating under pressure, transforming "no's" into opportunities, identifying and exploring hidden information.

Each chapter has been carefully thought out to add real value to your trading. With objective language and practical examples, this content was developed for sales professionals, negotiators and anyone looking to maximize their results through negotiation.

Therefore, I invite you to embark with me on this journey through the fascinating world of strategic trading. With each page, new doors of prosperity will open for you.

Let's start!

Yours sincerely

Reginaldo Osnildo

INTRODUCTION TO HIGH IMPACT NEGOTIATION: UNDERSTANDING THE FUNDAMENTALS OF EFFECTIVE NEGOTIATION

Welcome to our book on advanced trading strategies to maximize your results. This first chapter serves as a solid introduction to the fundamentals of effective negotiation.

Before we dive into the more complex tactics and techniques in the next chapters, it is essential to build a foundation of knowledge about the core elements of any successful negotiation. By mastering these fundamentals, you will be able to navigate tense discussions, deal with challenging personalities, and close profitable deals even in difficult circumstances.

In this opening chapter, we will examine the following fundamental topics:

- The essence of negotiation and why mastering this skill is so valuable

- The 3 main objectives in any negotiation

- How to properly prepare to increase your chances of success

- 4 essential human qualities of skilled negotiators

- Understanding different trading styles

- How to quickly build trust with anyone

- Techniques to discover the real motivations and interests of the other party

- Tools to maintain emotional control under pressure

By the end of this chapter, you will have a robust mental map of the core elements involved in highly effective negotiation. These are the foundations on which we will build in the rest of our book. Therefore, I invite you to pay attention to each concept as they form the basis for mastering the art of negotiation.

Let's start by explaining the essence of this valuable skill...

THE ESSENCE OF NEGOTIATION: WHY IS IT ESSENTIAL?

Many people think of negotiation as a battle to "win" or "lose". As if there is a fixed prize on the table and each side is fighting to get the biggest slice.

But in reality, skillful negotiation involves a much more complex and subtle dance with the other party. Each side comes to the table with its own interests, priorities, insights, constraints, and relationships.

Effective negotiation recognizes this human complexity and seeks to satisfy both sides in the best possible way. Instead of defeating your opponent, the focus is on expanding the pie so that everyone wins.

Master negotiators understand that you can achieve much more by building bridges, establishing mutual trust, and understanding each other's motivations.

Furthermore, 10% to 15% of economic activity involves trading. Whether we're seeking a loan, negotiating working conditions, closing a big sale, or simply deciding where to have dinner, negotiation is closely integrated into almost everything we do. This is exactly why it has become such an essential human skill.

In an increasingly complex and competitive business world, knowing how to negotiate can mean the difference between success and failure. People who have mastered this art have a distinct advantage in all spheres of life.

Therefore, we can state that:

Skilled negotiation is the ability to interact effectively with others to reach mutually acceptable agreements and resolutions.

It is a critical human skill because it helps you:

- Get the results you want without alienating or harming other parties

- Build valuable and lasting relationships

- Avoid or resolve conflicts

- Progress in your career

Improve your interpersonal communications as a whole

Whether we are negotiating with colleagues, clients, partners or loved ones, this skill allows us to navigate the complex human landscapes that surround us to create win-win solutions.

Now that we understand why negotiation is so valuable, let's explore the 3 main goals that any excellent negotiator pursues.

THE 3 MAIN OBJECTIVES OF EVERY SKILLED NEGOTIATOR

In any negotiation, there are 3 central goals that we must seek to achieve to ensure a successful outcome:

- Understand the real needs and interests of other parties

- Build trust and mutual goodwill

- Reach an agreement that satisfies both sides

Let's analyze each of them in greater depth:

UNDERSTAND THE REAL NEEDS AND INTERESTS OF OTHER PARTIES

Many negotiations fail because the parties don't understand - or don't even ask about - each other's true motivations and needs. Instead, they are stuck only with their own interests.

Excellent negotiators reverse this tendency by asking lots of open-ended questions to reveal what is really driving the other party. They listen carefully to responses without judgment to gain candid insights.

Uncovering these hidden motivations allows them to come up with much more creative solutions that satisfy every interest on the table. Instead of just reacting to the other party's demands, they can now come up with entirely new proposals that meet the fundamental needs of both sides.

BUILD TRUST AND MUTUAL GOODWILL

Trust is the lubricant that allows any negotiation to flow smoothly. Without it, discussions become bogged down by suspicion, resentment, and ineffective communications.

Excellent negotiators actively build this trust by demonstrating genuine goodwill and integrity throughout the process.

They put themselves in the other party's shoes to understand them more deeply. Avoid antagonistic language that could alienate the other party. Build rapport by sharing insights and personal stories when appropriate. And they consistently demonstrate their trustworthiness by following through on every promise and commitment they make.

The result is an environment of mutual respect and trust in which creative solutions can flourish.

REACH AN AGREEMENT THAT SATISFIES BOTH SIDES

The ultimate goal of any negotiation is to reach an agreement acceptable to all parties involved. Without this, the entire interaction was a waste of time and resources.

Skilled negotiators keep this end result in mind during all discussions. They know they need to satisfy the other party's needs as well as their own if they want to secure a deal.

That's why they spend so much time understanding everyone's true interests and building collaborative relationships. When you take good care of these first two objectives, reaching a profitable resolution becomes much more viable and fluid.

Now that we've looked at these 3 core objectives, let's explore how to properly prepare before any big negotiation to maximize your chances of success.

DEEP PREPARATION: YOUR FOUNDATION FOR SUCCESS

Solid preparation is what separates average negotiators from exceptional negotiators. It is during these pre-discussion hours that you build your foundation of knowledge, strategy and confidence.

Unfortunately, most people don't devote enough time to this critical phase. They rely too much on their instincts and natural negotiation skills. While innate talent certainly helps, without adequate preparation you will be at a huge disadvantage against a more methodical opponent.

During your pre-preparation, some essential elements to cover include:

- Determine your core interests and priorities - What results do you absolutely must achieve? What areas are you willing to compromise?

- Do in-depth research on the other party - What are their goals, constraints and negotiation strategies? Can you discover any levers or angles to explore?

- Define your BATNA (BEST ALTERNATIVE TO NEGOTIATED AGREEMENT) - What is the best case scenario if you fail to reach a deal now?

- Describe initial agreement options to present

- Map out strategic questions to ask and gain key insights into their interests and priorities

- Prepare responses and strategies for difficult negotiation scenarios, demands and tactics

- Review your verbal and nonverbal communication to exhibit confidence and collaboration

When you dedicate these several hours beforehand to strategic reflection, deep analysis, and mental practice, your chances of success skyrocket. You enter the discussion by being the best prepared and therefore the most convincing negotiator at the table.

Now that we've looked at why solid preparation is so critical, let's explore the 4 core human qualities that every good negotiator should cultivate.

THE 4 FUNDAMENTAL HUMAN QUALITIES OF EXCELLENT NEGOTIATORS

In addition to mastering processes, strategies, and technical preparation, great negotiators also share certain essential personal attributes that make them so skilled. Specifically, there are 4 fundamental human qualities that you must make part of your negotiation matrix:

1 - Patience

2 - Insight

3 - Trust

4 - Integrity

PATIENCE IS THE KEY TO TRADING

Patience is vital for several reasons. First, complex negotiations often involve many prolonged rounds of discussions before a final agreement is finalized. Staying calm under this long tension is mentally demanding.

Patience also allows you to actively listen to the other party, walk in their shoes, and gain essential insights into their real motivations. Rushing the other person or the discussion will only result in superficial agreements or complete failures.

Furthermore, when heated disputes or hostile tactics arise from the other side, remaining patient prevents you from engaging in unproductive emotional reactions. You maintain control, remain rational, and can navigate these challenges with grace.

PERSPECTIVE IS THE VISION OF THE WHOLE

Having a sharp and strategic mind is what allows skilled negotiators to see angles, insights and solutions that other parties miss. They can quickly identify the fundamental interests, needs, motivations and concerns on both sides of the argument.

This insight gives them a much broader picture of the situation and possible paths to resolution. Instead of being stuck just defending their own interests, they can come up with creative proposals based on the parties' shared interests.

Your ability to think strategically is a huge asset in complex discussions with multiple variables at play. While others get lost in the details, you can stay focused on the big picture of an optimal solution.

TRUST IS THE BASIS OF EVERYTHING

Every major negotiation has moments of tension, conflict and uncertainty. Demonstrating confidence even in these turbulent times is absolutely vital. When you project confidence in your posture, tone of voice, and body language, it transfers directly to the other party.

In contrast, if you show weakness, hesitation, or desperation, the other party will instantly detect this and use it against you as leverage. Your chances of getting a good deal plummet.

Therefore, cultivating a calm demeanor, a powerful posture, and a calm but assertive voice will serve you well in any negotiation, no matter the challenges faced.

INTEGRITY IS WHAT BUILDS

Integrity builds the trust that lubricates successful negotiations. When people see that you are trustworthy, consistent, and fair, they are much more likely to disclose important information and consider creative resolutions.

Integrity negotiators avoid manipulative language or behaviors just to gain an advantage. Instead, they are completely transparent about their interests and are always willing to present fair options that satisfy both sides.

This ethical and respectful way of negotiating encourages the other party to respond in an equally collaborative way. Together, you can build trust, explore mutual interests, and reach solid win-win agreements.

Now that we've looked at the 4 fundamental human qualities, let's explore different negotiation styles so you can adapt your approach depending on the situation and the people involved.

UNDERSTANDING DIFFERENT NEGOTIATION STYLES

Just as we have unique learning, communication and leadership styles, we also negotiate in different ways. There is no universal "correct" approach – only the one best suited to the specific context and people you are interacting with.

Knowing the different negotiation styles gives you the flexibility to adapt efficiently to different situations:

DISTRIBUTIVE/POSITIONAL NEGOTIATION

In distributive negotiation, each side adopts opposing positions to defend its interests. For example, a buyer wants the lowest possible price for a used car, while the seller wants the highest.
Each party competes to "win" the biggest share.

While this may be an appropriate approach for some scenarios, it often leads to zero-sum outcomes in which one wins and the other loses. This undermines opportunities to explore mutual gains.

COOPERATIVE/INTEGRATIVE NEGOTIATION

The cooperative approach encourages both parties to collaborate to satisfy mutual interests at the table. Rather than competing over position, there is an honest effort to understand each other's fundamental needs and explore creative options that benefit all participants.

Open communication, empathy and a creative spirit are central components of this collaborative approach.

PRINCIPLES-BASED NEGOTIATION

Principles-based negotiation focuses on aligning discussions with core values of ethics, fairness and mutual respect. Rather than being locked into specific positions or demands, each side explores options that reflect what is the right thing to do given the circumstances.

For example, if a salary discussion is at a standstill between an employee and his or her manager, rather than insisting on absolutes, they can use guiding principles such as "Pay each person according to their qualifications, contributions, and hard work" to arrive at a value. fair.

This focus on principles helps depolarize antagonistic positions and open space for ethical solutions.

Regardless of your chosen negotiation style, building trust quickly and consistently with the other party is absolutely essential to your success. Let's explore some of the best tactics for establishing that trust early on.

BUILDING TRUST FAST WITH ANYONE

Effective trust starts with your first handshake, eye contact, and exchange of words. Like the critical 15 seconds of a first impression, your initial actions send strong signals about you to the other person.

Fortunately, a few simple tactics can help you establish credibility and trust instantly.

The first is to maintain firm eye contact, accompanied by a genuine smile. Looking into the other person's eyes (without staring) demonstrates your trust and sincerity.

Pair this with a warm smile that lights up your entire face, especially your eyes.

Then, the handshake should be warm, with medium to firm pressure (adjusted to that of the other person) for 2 to 3 seconds. This demonstrates your safety while respecting the other person's physical limits.

Your posture and body language also communicate very quickly whether you are open, relaxed and receptive. Keep your shoulders back, your chest open, and your posture aligned but not rigid during your interactions. Lean slightly toward the other person when necessary to demonstrate your focus and full engagement in the conversation.

Finally, what you verbalize in the first few minutes creates the foundation for mutual trust. Expressions like "it's great to meet you," "I look forward to our valuable discussions," and "I appreciate your willingness to meet with me" send quick positive signals.

By combining friendly, open body language, constant eye contact, and encouraging verbal affirmations, you quickly establish an essential initial layer of mutual trust and respect.

Now that we've covered some quick and easy ways to build interpersonal trust, let's explore techniques for uncovering the other party's hidden interests and priorities - key insights for creating powerful solutions.

DISCOVERING THE REAL INTERESTS AND MOTIVATIONS OF THE OTHER PARTY

One of the biggest mistakes negotiators make is assuming they already know what the other party wants or needs from the interaction. In fact, our assumptions often don't even come close to reality.

The only way to truly understand the other party's fundamental interests and priorities is to ask questions, listen carefully, and dig deep into the answers you receive.

But what kinds of questions reveal these hidden insights? And how can you encourage honest and complete responses?

Let's look at some best practices:

> - Ask open-ended questions that cannot be answered with a simple "Yes" or "No" - This forces the other party to provide more detail and context, revealing important nuances.

> - Demonstrate genuine curiosity and refrain from judging the responses you receive - Your insights will not be shared if the other party feels they are being evaluated.

- Follow the natural flow of the conversation, asking follow-up questions to delve deeper into certain aspects - Don't interrupt or abruptly change the subject - extensively explore a productive line of questioning.

- For really important topics, rephrase the person's response in your own words for confirmation - This avoids misinterpretations and demonstrates that you really "heard" what was said.

- Carefully observe the other party's body language and emotional tone during their responses - This provides additional insights beyond the words spoken.

Practicing these techniques requires mental discipline. Your natural tendency will be to project your own assumptions and interests onto the other party. But by putting your ego and assumptions aside to really listen to the other person's needs, your ability to create mutually beneficial solutions skyrockets.

Now that we understand how to reveal your interlocutor's hidden interests, let's explore some strategies for maintaining self-control in high-pressure situations.

PSYCHOLOGY OF NEGOTIATION: HOW TO UNDERSTAND AND INFLUENCE YOUR INTERLOCUTORS

In this chapter, we'll dive into the fascinating psychology behind effective trading.

Understanding the fundamentals of how the human mind works will empower you to better analyze, influence, and connect with anyone at the negotiating table.

Specifically, we will explore the critical areas:

- The most common psychological traps that harm negotiators

- How our mental state affects our decisions and judgments

- Principles of persuasion to influence results

- Motivational drivers: what really motivates each person

- Identifying and responding to different personality types

- Body language and microexpressions : reading nonverbal cues

- Creating behavioral synchrony with your interlocutor

Understanding these psychological dynamics will allow you to successfully navigate the complex human landscapes of negotiation.

So, without further ado, let's look at some mental traps we're all susceptible to.

AVOIDING THE PSYCHOLOGICAL TRAPS OF NEGOTIATION

Unfortunately, our brains are not designed for trading. They evolved to deal with physical threats, not complex business discussions.

Consequently, there are many psychological traps that can sabotage our best efforts to reach profitable agreements.

Two of these incredibly common mental traps are: confirmation bias and loss aversion. Let's analyze them in more detail:

CONFIRMATION BIAS

Our confirmation bias causes us to seek out, interpret, and give more weight to information that confirms our pre-existing beliefs. We then downplay or completely dismiss evidence that contradicts these beliefs.

Unfortunately, this hampers our negotiation skills. Unconsciously, we begin to filter everything the other party says against our current interests, even if their concerns are perfectly valid and reasonable.

This blocks our ability to genuinely understand them, hindering our ability to reach creative resolutions.

LOSS AVERSION

Our mental programming also makes us very loss averse. The stress and mental pain of losing something is much greater than the equal pleasure of gaining something.

This leads to more extreme and inflexible demands and positions, making progress at the negotiating table more difficult. We don't want to give an inch if there is a chance the other party will take advantage of it and make more gains at our expense.

Understanding these irrational biases allows us to mitigate them with full awareness. We can strive to listen to divergent perspectives and be more open to conciliatory options where everyone wins something rather than insisting that our side wins everything.

Now that we've covered some common psychological pitfalls, let's examine how your mental state impacts your performance.

YOUR MENTAL STATE PROFOUNDLY INFLUENCES YOUR JUDGMENTS

Have you ever felt mentally drained, hungry, or distracted by stress during an important negotiation?

Most people answer "yes" - and pay a price for it.

Research shows that variables such as inadequate sleep, fatigue and stress can significantly impair our executive planning, focusing and decision-making abilities. Acting impulsively based on emotions becomes much more likely.

Likewise, low glucose levels due to long intervals without eating can leave us irritable and prone to poor choices.

This clearly demonstrates how crucial it is to take care of your body and mind before any significant trading.

When your mental and physical state is optimal, you are much better equipped to listen carefully, control your emotions, think creatively, and make the right strategic decisions under pressure.
Therefore, whenever possible, ensure that you:

- Get enough sleep the night before

- Eat a nutritious meal

- Exercise to release endorphins

- Reduce other stresses before important interaction

Your mental lucidity and energy will make a big difference in the quality of the results achieved.

Now that we understand how our internal state influences our negotiations, let's learn about some proven principles of persuasion.

PRINCIPLES OF PERSUASION: INFLUENCED THOUGHTS AND DECISIONS

There is real science behind the ability to influence and persuade others. Understanding and applying some fundamental principles of social psychology can make a big difference in how effective you are in negotiations.

PRINCIPLE OF RECIPROCITY

People tend to respond to the treatment they receive from others. If you show confidence, they will reciprocate with confidence. Show toughness, and you will receive the same in return.

Therefore, enter into a negotiation with respect, good humor and openness of mind to encourage the same reciprocal behavior in the other person. This sets the tone for a much more productive cooperative discussion.

PRINCIPLE OF COHERENCE

Once people verbally commit to a decision or course of action, however small, they feel obligated to behave in a manner consistent with that commitment.

Then, as a negotiation unfolds, reveal areas of agreement and ask the other party to verbalize that alignment. This makes it much more likely that they will "walk the walk" when it comes time to finalize the actual deal.

PRINCIPLE OF AUTHORITY

External symbols of authority – titles, dress, body language of power – have an automatic effect on our decisions. We have an innate tendency to respect the influence of legitimate "authorities".

You can take advantage of this by dressing appropriately for each negotiation and adopting a posture and tone of voice that project competence and credibility.

The most critical aspect of success in any negotiation is your ability to connect, understand and influence the other party. Psychology provides powerful insights into how to do just that, allowing you to shape more favorable outcomes.

Now that we understand some general principles of influence, let's dive deeper into what really motivates each person and how we can use that to our advantage.

MOTIVATIONAL DRIVERS: UNDERSTANDING WHAT REALLY MOTIVATES EACH PERSON

To customize your negotiation approach for greater effectiveness, it is essential to understand the core drivers or motivations that guide each person's behavior.

Fortunately, from decades of research, psychologists have identified 6 fundamental human needs that drive and influence us all to varying degrees.

Are they:

- Power

- Realization

- Affiliation

- Security

- Tradition

- Fun

Let's explore them in more depth:

POWER

Power-motivated individuals want to control outcomes and exert influence. They often adopt aggressive, assertive and sometimes manipulative approaches depending on the context.

REALIZATION

Achievement-oriented people are focused on improving and succeeding against some standard of excellence. They generally adopt rational strategies and are willing to take moderate or calculated risks.

AFFILIATION

Those who value affiliation above all else seek warm personal connections. They prioritize working cooperatively, in groups, avoiding conflicts whenever possible to maintain a harmonious environment.

SECURITY

Psychological, physical and financial security are the greatest needs of this group. They tend to be risk averse and seek stability over potentially greater but uncertain rewards.

TRADITION

Those who value existing traditions and structures try to preserve the current order of things. They strongly resist rapid changes or disruptions to "the way things have always been done."

FUN

Finally, some people are simply motivated by fun, variety, and constant stimulation. They want every interaction to be dynamic and energized. They hate boredom above all else.

Mapping which of these drivers most strongly guides the other party allows you to customize your communication and influencing style for much greater effectiveness. You can choose examples, stories, and calls to action that resonate deeply with the core values of that person or audience.

This makes it much easier to gain alignment, influence thoughts and shape decisions in your favor. So pay careful attention and identify which drivers motivate each person you are trying to persuade or negotiate with. Personalizing your approach to following could be the key to your success.

Now that we understand these 6 internal drivers, let's explore how to strategically identify and respond to different personality types in negotiation.

DEALING EFFECTIVELY WITH CHALLENGING PERSONALITIES

In every negotiation, you will eventually encounter complicated personalities that test your limits.

Fortunately, psychology has identified 5 extremely common behavioral profiles that you are likely to encounter at the negotiating table.

Understanding these profiles will allow you to plan personalized strategies to deal diplomatically with each of them.

The 5 most common profiles are:

- The talker

- The stubborn

- The suspicious

- The indecisive

- The distracted

Let's deconstruct each of them:

THE SPEAKER

Talkers don't stop talking. They dominate the conversation, interrupt others and rarely listen. To deal with them:

- Politely interrupt them to ask your own question or raise a concern.

- Set strict time limits for each person to speak.

- Be concise when speaking; Long explanations will make them interrupt.

THE STUBBORN

Stubborn people are inflexible and insist on irrelevant points just on principle. To influence them:

- Listen to them patiently to build rapport

- Rephrase your arguments to show that you understand

- Highlight areas of agreement before discussing differences

- Ask lots of open-ended questions to understand all perspectives

THE DISCONFUSING

Suspicious people assume bad intentions from others. They are overly skeptical and resistant. To earn your trust:

- Be extremely transparent by sharing processes and plans

- Only make statements that you can prove with concrete facts

- Demonstrate your character and competence consistently through actions

THE UNDECISION

Indecisive people are afraid of making the "wrong" decision and procrastinate or avoid it. To help them move forward:

- Segment big decisions into smaller, more manageable steps

- Provide multiple options along with pros and cons

- Set deadlines to gain clarity and closure

THE DISTRACTED

Distracted people have difficulty paying attention; your thoughts wander. To keep them focused:

- Make frequent eye contact

- Ask open-ended questions that require deeper insights

- Summarize the main points covered and agreed

Mastering these challenging personalities will make you a much more skillful and influential negotiator. You'll be confident in dealing with virtually anyone at the negotiating table!

So far, we have focused entirely on verbal communication. But, body language conveys powerful insights to trained negotiators. It's time to learn how to decode these nonverbal signals!

READING THE CLUES OF BODY LANGUAGE AND MICROEXPRESSIONS

Your literal words are just a fraction of the total communication. According to psychology professor emeritus Albert Mehrabian , effective face-to-face communication of emotions or attitudes involves three central elements: nonverbal behavior (facial expressions, for example), tone of voice, and the literal meaning of the spoken word. He believes that these three essential elements explain how we convey our liking or disliking for another person. He concluded that only 7% of a message's meaning is conveyed by words, while tone of voice accounts for 38% and body language for 55% of message perception. Therefore, paying attention to the "between the lines" of what the other person's body is signaling gives them critical insights beyond what is being said.

Let's look at some important signs to watch out for:

- Sustained eye contact generally indicates trust and honest engagement in the conversation. Constantly looking away can indicate shame, discomfort, or even potential deception.

- Genuine smiles involve the eyes, resulting in "crow's feet" at the corners. Fake smiles only involve the mouth.

- Leaning towards you shows interest. Leaning back denotes a more defensive or confrontational attitude.

- Legs and feet turned towards you indicate receptivity. Turning feet or entire body away (particularly with arms crossed) signals a desire to exit the interaction.

In addition to these general behaviors, there are also fleeting emotional "micro-moments" called micro-expressions. They only last fractions of a second, but they accurately deliver the other person's real emotions.

Body language masters can read this extra layer of emotional information and use it to guide influence or problem-solving strategies. Therefore, pay attention to the signals your interlocutor is sending in addition to the words being said. This gives you valuable insights.

Speaking of the importance of body language, there are also proven techniques for creating behavioral alignment with your counterpart, leading to more trust and positive influence.

CREATING BEHAVIORAL "MIRRORING"

Mirroring or reflecting the other person's body language is a powerful technique for subconsciously establishing a stronger connection and influence during negotiations.

Research shows that when you replicate someone's gestures, facial expressions, mannerisms, and even breathing pattern, they unconsciously perceive you as similar to them. This triggers more positive feelings and receptivity to your ideas and requests.

This is why mirror body language works so well as an influence tool. You can mirror behaviors like:

- Head tilt angle

- Posture and hand gestures

- Speech speed and vocal tone

- Facial expressions such as raising eyebrows

Initially, try to reflect one behavior at a time until it becomes natural. With frequent practice, you will be able to mirror a series of simultaneous mannerisms to create deep alignment.

Remember that this technique only works when done with genuine intention to connect more deeply with your interlocutor.

Now that we understand the science behind influencing others, it's time to apply that knowledge to explore some of the advanced negotiation strategies and techniques available to you.

Together, we have already built a solid foundation understanding human psychology and its implications for successful interactions. In the next chapters, I will equip you with specific practical skills to master your important trades from now on.

So turn the page and let's continue our journey!

MIRRORING TECHNIQUES: BUILDING RAPPORT AND ESTABLISHING TRUST QUICKLY

Building a strong personal connection and trust with someone quickly is not easy. It requires focused and intentional strategies.

Fortunately, as we will see in this chapter, the "mirroring" technique provides a proven shortcut for establishing this crucial rapport in minutes.

Specifically, we'll explore:

- What is mirroring and how does it generate interpersonal influence

- The subtle ways to mirror body linguistics, voice and more

- When and when not to use mirroring in your trading

- Practicing fluid mirroring through structured exercises

Mastering this skill will fundamentally change your ability to create meaningful personal connections quickly and influence outcomes more easily.

So, without further ado, let's dive into the power of mirroring!

WHAT IS MIRRORING AND HOW DOES IT GENERATE INFLUENCE?

Mirroring refers to the subtle imitation of another person's verbal and nonverbal behavior during social interactions. This includes reflecting body posture, gestures, tone of voice, speech and more.

When done well, mirroring generates influence for a few powerful reasons:

- Sends automatic signals of similarity between you. Subconsciously, people are more attracted to and influenced by those perceived as similar. Therefore, the more you mirror someone's standards, the closer they will feel to you.

- Mirroring demonstrates your focus and total interest in the other. You literally become a reflection of your behaviors, satisfying your inherent desire to be heard and understood. This makes them much more receptive to your ideas and perspectives as well.

- Promotes the release of the social bonding hormones oxytocin and serotonin. This makes the other person physiologically happier, more relaxed and open to a positive relationship.

- It signals that you are a highly empathetic and socially attuned "mirror person". Again, these are qualities that naturally generate trust and goodwill.

Now that we understand the power of this unique interpersonal influence technique, let's explore exactly how to effectively mirror others.

HOW TO STRATEGICALLY MIRROR GESTURES, VOICE AND BEHAVIORS

There are countless subtle ways to mirror your interlocutor during a conversation. Let's analyze the main areas where to apply this:

- **Body language:** mirror hand/arm gestures, body tilts, posture, foot/leg orientation and more. For example, if they lean forward while speaking, do the same.

- **Vocal intonation and vocabulary:** reflect the emotional tone, volume, rhythm of speech and even word choice. If they sound excited and speak quickly, match that. If they use formal corporate language, do the same.

- **Facial expressions:** reproduce your smiles, eyebrow raises, mouth grimaces and other facial micro-moments. As they say, " **IMITATION** is the greatest form of flattery!"

- **Breathing patterns:** pay attention to their resting breathing rhythm. You can slightly mirror this as well for greater physical alignment.

Ideally, choose **ONE** of your behaviors to reflect on at a time, rather than trying to imitate everything simultaneously at first. This will look artificial.

As each mirrored behavior becomes more natural, you can expand your repertoire until you cover all linguistic areas fluidly and imperceptibly.

WHEN TO USE (AND NOT USE) MIRRORING TECHNIQUES

Like any powerful tool of influence, mirroring can be used for both good and evil. So here are some guidelines to keep it ethical:

✓ **Use to establish positive rapport :** the main purpose should be to create sincere connections and mutual understanding.

✗ **Do not use it to manipulate results:** respect the free choice and autonomy of others. Never mirror just to force an agreement.

✓ **Maintain process integrity:** Be 100% authentic about your interests and limitations during negotiations.

✗ **Cease if the other party feels uncomfortable:** Some people may view intense mirroring as invasive. Be attentive and respect limits.

In general, before mirroring someone, ask yourself, "Is my intention here noble? Am I acting respectfully and with the best intentions?" If the answer is yes, move on.

Okay, now that we understand **WHEN** to apply this skill, let's practice **HOW to** mirror fluidly through some quick exercises.

PRACTICING FLUID MIRRORING

Practice time! Here are 3 simple yet powerful exercises to improve your mirroring techniques:

Exercise #1 - Mirroring a video

- Pull up any speech or YouTube video with someone talking for a few minutes. Focus on **ONE** area of body language at a time to mirror fluidly.

- For example, hand and arm gestures. Or tilt and orientation of the body. Or facial expressions.

- Do this for 5-10 minutes, then reset your focus to another area of body language.

Exercise #2 - Mirroring a partner in real time

- Do this workout face to face with a friend or colleague. Ask them to speak freely for a few minutes about a random topic while you subtly mirror one of their verbal or nonverbal behaviors at a time.

- Then, switch roles! This helps you notice which mannerisms are more easily imitated and which ones need more practice.

Exercise #3 - Recording and evaluating yourself

- Videotape yourself imitating a famous speech from an inspirational leader, influential politician or iconic business persona.

- Watch the video afterwards, analyzing which behaviors you naturally mirrored well and where there are still opportunities for improvement.

- By dedicating just 10 to 15 minutes a day to these exercises, you will soon master the subtle art of quick and influential mirroring.

Remember, time and intentional practice are the keys! Don't give up too soon before these mirroring behaviors become second nature to you.

Now equipped with this powerful new social tool, you'll be in a much better position to establish trusting relationships quickly and influence others more easily.

Please use this skill wisely to positively impact more lives!

In the next chapter, we'll dive into another critical human skill for successful negotiators: the ability to cultivate and communicate genuine empathy.

I hope you continue following this journey with us to fully master the skills necessary to maximize negotiation results!

THE ART OF TACTICAL EMPATHY: USING EMOTIONAL UNDERSTANDING TO ADVANCE IN NEGOTIATIONS

Empathy - the ability to put yourself in another person's shoes and genuinely feel their emotions - is one of the most valuable human skills in any context.

And in negotiations, demonstrating strategic empathy for your interlocutor can be the decisive key to unlocking impasses, building trust and shaping mutually beneficial agreements.

In this chapter, we will delve into:

- Why empathy is so essential to successful negotiation

- How to cultivate a highly empathetic mindset

- Communication techniques to express this empathy effectively

- Avoiding empathy pitfalls such as excessive personal pain

- Setting healthy boundaries for yourself while still remaining deeply in tune with others

So, get ready to delve into the power of sincere emotional connection and how to apply it for tangible results at the negotiating table!

Starting with the basics, let's explore why this primordial human skill of empathy is so crucial.

WHY IS EMPATHY SO ESSENTIAL TO SUCCESS?

The ability to genuinely put yourself in someone else's shoes, connecting on a deep emotional level to understand their most authentic concerns, fears, and needs, is so valuable for several compelling reasons:

First, it encourages the other party to open up more and freely share crucial information that would otherwise remain hidden. When people feel deeply understood, their natural guard drops.

Second, empathy helps you understand the other party's true interests and motivations. You gain insights that go far beyond what is just being said at the table, allowing for more creative and personalized negotiation strategies.

Third, it creates a climate of trust, goodwill and mutual respect. The other party notices your genuine care and concern for their well-being, even if the two of you don't agree on everything. This builds positive common ground.

And finally, when you demonstrate consistently high levels of integrity, sensitivity, and emotional understanding, it becomes a powerful model that encourages the other party to respond with equal openness and collaboration.

Therefore, prioritizing sincere connection and the ability to put yourself in the other party's shoes will serve you tremendously well in your most challenging negotiations.

Now that we understand the **VALUE** of empathy, let's explore how to develop a highly empathetic mindset as a negotiator.

CULTIVATING A DEEPLY EMPATHIC MENTALITY

The good news is that empathy can be intentionally cultivated by anyone willing to increase their self-awareness and take regular training.

Here are some proven best practices:

- Always remember that each person is the protagonist of their own life story. They are the heroes of their journey, just like you. This helps you see your perspectives as equally valid.

- Try to vividly visualize the life situations that have shaped your current mindsets. How have their past experiences, education, relationships and successes or traumas made them who they are today?

- In conversations, focus all your attention on listening deeply and understanding your interlocutors before making any response. Eliminate distractions, make eye contact, and listen with genuine intent to learn their unique paradigms.

- Temporarily suspend your ego and self-interest. Instead of filtering statements through the lens of what you stand to gain or lose, simply focus on deeply understanding their perspectives.

- Periodically verbalize what you are hearing and how you understand they are feeling. Ask follow-up questions to sharpen your understanding and signal active mentalization. Phrasing what was said in your own words demonstrates that you have truly absorbed the emotional essence.

The more you practice this mental muscle of empathy through these exercises, the stronger these neural connections become. Eventually, it becomes a trait incorporated into your overall personality.

Now, in addition to **CULTIVATING** an empathetic mindset, we also need to practice **COMMUNICATING** our emotional understanding effectively during real interactions.

COMMUNICATING YOUR EMPATHY EFFECTIVELY

Cultivating a highly empathetic mindset is the first step. But to influence negotiation outcomes, you also need to proactively signal this sensitivity to your interlocutors through your words and actions.

Here are some best practices to make you skilled:

- Maintain solid eye contact while they are speaking to convey complete focus and interest. Gently nod your head to encourage opening.

- Subtly mirror their body language to establish subconscious alignment. For example, adopt similar posture and hand gestures.

- Paraphrase the main points of pain and frustration to confirm that you have captured the emotional essence. "It seems like you were quite upset when..."

- Make direct statements validating their feelings. "It's very understandable to feel betrayed in this situation. I would feel that way too..."

- Always demonstrate goodwill by assuming their best intentions, even when you disagree. "I know your concerns come from a place of caring deeply about your team..."

- When applicable, express when you have already experienced challenges, emotions or similar situations. This generates even deeper shared experiential understanding.

Again, when they feel like you understand them and genuinely care, their defenses lower. They respond with greater goodwill, a willingness to collaborate, and even shared emotional vulnerability.

This deeper level of connection and trust opens doors to explore creative solutions that transcend rigid positions and serve the core interests of everyone involved.

AVOIDING TRAPS: DON'T ASSUME OTHER PEOPLE'S PAIN

Now, while cultivating deeper levels of emotional understanding for the other parties during negotiation, it is important not to "take on" someone else's pain too much, to the point of harming your own well-being.

Unfortunately, compassionate negotiators sometimes unconsciously absorb the emotional stress or trauma of others. Psychologists call this "empathic pain."

While noble in intention, in the long run it can lead to compassion fatigue, mental exhaustion, and even poor physical health.

So when projecting empathy, remember these healthy boundaries:

  ✓ Listen deeply and seek to understand their unique perspectives

  ✗ Don't take your negative emotions personally

✓ Acknowledge and validate your feelings

✗ Don't try to solve or fix your pain

✓ Compassionately offer your unconditional support

✗ Don't go into rescue mode or over-engage

At the end of the day, you can't control anyone else's choices or heal anyone else's pain - only gently share your support and wisdom.

So, do your part by being a present empathetic listener. But don't also take on the emotional burden that isn't yours to carry. Just squeeze the other party's shoulders with compassion - don't try to carry them completely for them.

And with that, we conclude our deep dive into the power of sincere emotional connection and how to apply it strategically in challenging negotiations.

In the next chapter, we'll move on to a new set of advanced strategies to help you reset the narrative when you face difficult impasses, seemingly irretrievable disagreements, or unacceptable demands.

Until then, I wish you the best on your journeys of continued self-reflection and growth!

MASTERING THE "NO": TRANSFORMING REJECTIONS INTO OPPORTUNITIES

Few things are as discouraging during a negotiation as hearing the other party say "no."

Especially when it seems categorical, definitive and impossible to get around.

However, master negotiators view "no" only as the beginning of a new productive phase of the conversation... not the end of it. The key is to have a plan to turn that initial rejection into eventual progress.

In this chapter, you'll learn how to do just that through tested tactics to:

- Mentally redefine the meaning of "no"

- Politely challenge limiting assumptions behind it

- Ask open-ended questions to reveal hidden concerns

- Finding new options that transcend the initial binary rejection

So, get ready to master "no" and transform apparent impasses into bridges to shared success. Let's start!

UNDERSTANDING THE LAYERS OF MEANING BEHIND "NO"

The first key to effectively dealing with a negative is understanding that there are layers of meaning behind it.

Specifically, the other party is communicating one of these 3 levels of message when saying no:

- **Level 1 - Refusal of current proposal:** "No, I do not agree with this specific suggestion you just presented." This is simply a rejection of the individual option placed on the table, not necessarily a dismissal of the entire broader issue.

- **Level 2 - Signaling a deeper concern:** "There is some undisclosed problem or unmet need behind this no." This is where the real opportunity is hidden! Delving deeper into these concerns expands new possibilities.

- **Level 3 - Unwillingness to negotiate:** "I absolutely refuse to consider other perspectives or work towards a solution." This deeper, more abrasive level of rejection often arises from trust issues. Building rapport by defusing the situation can reopen their minds.

So whenever you hear "no", first determine which of these 3 levels is truly at play. From there, you can strategically calibrate your response to advance the conversation.

Let's explore some of the best tactics for each scenario.

STRATEGIES TO DEAL WITH EACH LEVEL OF "NO"

Now that we understand the deeper meanings and motivations behind a denial, let's dive into tactical approaches to dealing with each level:

Responding to Level 1 "No"

When someone rejects your initial proposal or request but remains open to the general idea, there are some effective responses:

> **- Politely probe the underlying reasoning:** "I can understand why this approach didn't seem ideal to you. Tell me more about your specific concerns with it."

> **- Suggest modified versions:** "How about a slightly different version like this...?"

> **- Commit gradually:** "Okay, what if we removed this problematic element from the suggestion but kept the rest? Does that seem more feasible?"

Responding to Level 2 "No"

Sometimes a superficial No hides deeper concerns that, once resolved, remove barriers to agreement. To reveal them, respond like this:

- **Investigate with sincere curiosity:** "Help me better understand what concerns you in this specific scenario."

- **Ask open-ended questions and listen carefully to the answers** to gain clarity and nuance your own perspectives.

- **Rephrase the main points to confirm that you have captured their central concerns** and, if necessary, ask for additional clarification.

Once the underlying issue is fully understood, **only then suggest options** that address that genuine pain or need.

Responding to Level 3 "No"

When someone isn't at all open to changing their mind or considering alternatives, adopt these tactics:

- **Don't force the issue now.** Take a break and suggest resuming the discussion later when emotions are calmer.

- **Focus on rebuilding the relationship** , mutual trust and respect by sharing perspectives in a non-threatening way.

- Look for interests, values, or experiences that you share to generate common ground first.

- Once this fundamental human connection has been established again, **propose to restart the negotiation** with open dialogue and good faith.

Remember, when someone's defenses are too high, resolving the immediate issue is secondary to reestablishing respect and mental availability first.

ADDITIONAL TOOLS FOR DEALING WITH REJECTIONS

In addition to these situational tactics, there are also some useful general tools for dealing with negatives:

YES... AND " technique - reconcile, recognize, escalate

Example:

" **YES** , I understand your reluctance with this billing model **... And** would it be possible to consider an alternative structure like this...?"

- Bring a 3rd neutral option

When stuck between two options, present a new one that transcends the current impasse.

- Focus on higher common interests

"I believe we all want what's best for the company/clients/employees long-term. How can we achieve that?"

In general, view "no" as the start of real dialogue. Master it by patiently persisting to understand the fears behind it and come up with creative options that resolve them.

And remember, if after your best effort the other party still refuses to cooperate, you always have the option of simply walking away from the situation. It's not a failure - just a sign that it's not a productive match.

Keep trying to influence in good faith. But also know the right time to move forward amicably. You can't control other people's openness - only yours.

Either way, I hope this new perspective, tools, and strategies help you skillfully navigate the challenging territory of "no" and turn it into new paths of progress!

THE POWER OF STRATEGIC QUESTIONS: DIRECTING NEGOTIATION WITH KEY QUESTIONS

Skillful questions are the master tool for influencing negotiations in your favor. As the old saying goes:

"Questions are the answer"

Knowing **WHAT** questions to ask, **WHEN** to ask them, and **HOW** to answer them effectively shapes the entire discussion toward the outcome you want.

In this chapter, we'll dive into the power of this simple yet elegant instrument, exploring:

- The science of why questions are so persuasive

- Different types of strategic questions

- Optimal times for high-impact questions

- Tactics for answering questions masterfully

- Practicing asking powerful questions

So get ready to master this fundamental skill that separates excellent negotiators from the rest of the pack!

THE SCIENCE BEHIND THE POWER OF GOOD QUESTIONS

Why are well-crafted questions so persuasive in changing minds and driving results?

The psychology behind this is fascinating and boils down to this:

- They focus attention and dialogue on the areas that most benefit your case

- They politely challenge the other party's limiting assumptions

- They extract crucial insights into undisclosed motivations, values and goals

In other words, skillful questions shape the entire mental arena in your favor.

They determine the topics discussed, the perspectives considered, and the criteria by which proposals are evaluated. This organically channels the conversation towards your desired outcome.

Additionally, well-formulated questions **DEMONSTRATE** your genuine focus on understanding the other party and finding the best way forward together. This builds trust and goodwill.

Now that we understand **WHY** questions work, let's explore the main strategic **TYPES** for influencing discussions.

SIX POWERFUL STRATEGIC QUESTIONS

Although hundreds of variations exist, these 6 categories capture the main question "moves" that shape negotiations:

- *Clarification questions*

    Example: "Can you explain what you meant by...?"

    Purpose: Obtain additional details and context.

- *Guess Questions*

    Example: "How would you react if we did X...?"

    Purpose: Obtain informed answers and commitment to potential scenarios.

- *Challenge Questions*

    Example: "What would need to change in our approach for you to approve...?"

    Purpose: Politely challenge preconceived notions and identify solutions.

- *Emotional Connection Questions*

Example: "What worries you most about this scenario?"

Purpose: Build trust and goodwill through deeper empathetic understanding.

- *Framing questions*

Example: "Our goal here should be to ensure the most positive outcome possible for all parties - do you agree?"

Purpose: Establish shared criteria and values for evaluating options and making decisions.

- *Closing questions*

Example: "Considering these benefits we discussed, would you be willing to approve this agreement now?"

Purpose: Ask for commitment and close the deal.

Keeping these core categories in mind helps you formulate strategies for asking targeted, impactful questions for each stage of the negotiation.

But besides **KNOWING** what types of questions to ask, **TIMING** is also everything. So let's look at what crucial **MOMENTS** you should come in with your best questions.

DECISIVE MOMENTS TO ASK HIGH IMPACT QUESTIONS

While strategic questions should be sprinkled throughout the conversation, there are specific occasions when they are particularly influential in shaping the overall course of the negotiation.

Here are 5 crucial moments to leverage:

- Right at the beginning of the interaction

> Start by probing the terrain with some fundamental mapping questions to quickly and strategically determine the big picture you are facing before formulating proposals.

> Examples:

>> "I'd like to start by better understanding your priorities and essential requirements on this project - can you tell me more about them?"

>> "What are the most important metrics by which you will evaluate the options we will discuss today?"

- After making your initial proposal

Once you've presented an initial proposal or plan, immediately ask powerful questions to read their response, position advantages, and overcome objections as early as possible.

Examples:

"Given these capabilities I've highlighted, what seems most valuable in our approach to you?"

"Considering your previously stated objectives, where do you see my proposal meeting or not meeting your key needs?"

- When *you feel resistance or skepticism*

As soon as you detect any hesitation or disagreement, step in with motivating questions designed to dispel concerns and rebuild positive alignment.

Examples:

"It sounds like some of this approach made you uncomfortable - can you tell me more about your concerns so I can address them directly?"

"What would help us modify some of these elements to get your full approval?"

- *When they are ready to decide*

As the negotiation reaches the final stages, focus your questions on confirming willingness, resolving final details, and closing the deal.

Examples:

"Considering all the evidence and benefits we discussed on my side, as well as the concessions on your side, are you ready to move and finalize this deal now?"

"Are there any final steps or contingencies we need to cover before we confirm this?"

- *During moments of impasse*

If negotiations stall due to seemingly irreconcilable disagreements or heightened emotions, pause and reevaluate with a few crucial questions.

Examples:

"We seem to have reached a point where we can't see eye to eye. Let's take a step back - what can each of us do to reestablish some common ground here?"

"Are there compromises or compromise options not yet considered that we can explore?"

Mastering these key question moments transforms you from a passive negotiator into a proactive strategist completely shaping discussions.

Now, it is very important to not only ask good questions, but to respond skillfully when the roles are reversed too! So let's look at some techniques for this too.

ANSWERING QUESTIONS LIKE A MASTER

Just like your questions, your answers also impressively determine where the negotiation goes next. So here are some guidelines for responding like an expert:

- Listen to the entire question carefully without interrupting

- Reflect for 2-3 seconds before responding - don't rush

- Start by agreeing with any valid point or premise in the question before contradicting the rest

- Focus your answers on the benefits of your proposal - not just the features

- Limit the use of "no, but..." as this minimizes and antagonizes

- If a question is irrelevant or based on false information, reconstruct the context first

Again, the goal should be to direct each interaction into more positive and productive territory. Your skillful responses make this possible.

Ready to put these diverse strategies and powerful question insights to immediate use? Excellent! Let's practice and formulate some to improve this critical skill...

PRACTICE ASKING STRATEGIC QUESTIONS

Now it's your turn to create.

Answer these 5 questions I asked you with your own strategic questions:

- *Question 1: What are your biggest priorities in this project?*

    Your strategic question:

...

- Question 2: Why doesn't our service adequately meet your needs?

Your strategic question:

...

- Question 3: In what areas would you need to see changes to approve this proposal?

Your strategic question:

...

- Question 4: What still worries you about working with us?

Your strategic question:

...

- Question 5: Given all the evidence I have provided, will you sign this contract today?

Your strategic question:

...

Great! Formulating these impactful questions taking into account context and strategic objectives is the key to masterfully directing negotiations.

I hope you continue to practice and master this fundamental instrument that all successful traders share!

NEGOTIATION UNDER PRESSURE: STAYING CALM AND IN CONTROL IN CHALLENGING SITUATIONS

Intense negotiations invariably generate moments of extreme pressure.

Maybe an impossible deadline is approaching. Or unreasonable demands from the other party. Or your proposal being torn to pieces in front of an audience.

Whatever the cause, tension quickly rises and threatens to take you out of your center of peace, lucidity and strategic control.

In this chapter, we'll explore how to stay centered under heavy fire through techniques to:

- Mentally redefine stress as an ally

- Proactive release of physiological tension

- Focusing your breathing and attention on the present moment

- Calmly demonstrating confidence and control no matter what

- Disarming pressure tactics through calm assertiveness

So, get ready to conquer stress and perform masterfully under the brightest spotlight!

REDEFINING STRESS AS A POSITIVE CATALYST

The first key to flourishing under pressure is understanding that stress itself doesn't have to be your enemy. In fact, it can be your greatest ally if you approach it correctly.

You see, that tightness in the throat, sweaty palms, and racing heart are automatic, evolved physiological reactions to imminent physical danger.

Our body is instinctively preparing to fight, flee or freeze. But for modern trading, this is not the most useful answer.

So instead of wishing these sensations would go away, accept them as positive excitement and redirect that energy into a state of intense presence and directed focus.

Keep that physical sensitivity sharp, but purify it mentally for a higher purpose - to master this situation with wisdom and grace.

In other words, acknowledge the fire, but purify it from raw emotional fuel to the concentrated elegance of a candle flame—equally intense but infinitely more controllable.

This will keep you sharp and ready for the challenge without becoming mentally clouded by tension.

PROACTIVE DISCHARGE TECHNIQUES FOR PHYSIOLOGICAL TENSION

Now that we have mentally redefined stress as our ally, we also need to proactively deal with its physical manifestation in our bodies.

If all that nervous energy gets stuck in and partying, you'll end up acting impulsively or even unintentionally aggressively.

Therefore, consciously release any muscular tension or nervousness through:

- Prolonged exhalations to calm your sympathetic nervous system

- Vigorously shake or gently stretch your fingers and other extremities

- Contract intensely and then relax each muscle group, starting from the feet to the head

Releasing this anxious energy in a controlled way will prevent it from accidentally spilling over into counterproductive outbursts of intense emotions.

Instead, you remain a quiet source of calm under pressure - capable of strategic clarity and steady influence regardless of the turmoil around you.

ANCHORING YOURSELF IN THE PRESENT MOMENT THROUGH FOCUSED ATTENTION

In addition to resetting tension mentally and releasing it physically, it's also vital that you ground yourself firmly in the present moment.

If your mind starts to wander to possible bad outcomes or you get stuck recalling past mistakes, your anxiety and fear will only increase.

Therefore, use these situational anchors to ground your awareness in the now:

- Focus your breathing - feel the air moving in and out of your body

- Gently squeeze your thumb and index finger together to feel this sensation

- Look deeply into other people's eyes when talking to them

- Listen carefully without judgment to everything that is being said

This state of intense presence stops you from slipping into unproductive thoughts about the past or future. Your focus is on the immediate interaction in front of you.

This calm lucidity allows you to respond to the moment with flexibility and maturity, not with fixed patterns of pre-programmed behaviors.

RADIATING CONFIDENCE AND CONTROL NO MATTER WHAT

Remember, your posture, body language and presence communicate just as loudly as your actual words.

Therefore, regardless of the internal storm you may be feeling, your external behavior should remain a rock of calm and confidence for others to lean on.

Here are some quick tips for designing silent control under pressure:

- Upright posture and shoulders back

- Chin parallel to the floor

- Firm eye contact

- Calm, rhythmic tone of voice

- Deep abdominal breathing

- Neutral facial expression or slight smile

Remember, emotions are contagious. If you can calmly instill confidence through your body language, this will spread to others too, often completely defusing high-pressure situations.

CALM ASSERTIVENESS TO DISABLE PRESSURE TACTICS

In moments when people are clearly trying to apply unfair or manipulative pressure on you, respond with calm assertiveness.

This means establishing fair limits but without antagonism. For example:

> "I understand your urgency in this decision, but I don't feel we have all the necessary information yet. We will explore options that best serve the interests of both parties."

This firm approach prevents you from being pushed around without arousing equally counterproductive defense in the other party. You skillfully redirect the conversation to more productive terrain.

And remember, if even calm assertiveness fails, you always have the right to remove yourself from the situation completely. There is no need to absorb unnecessary abuse just to "seal the deal."

Sometimes strategic withdrawal by a future date is the only way to de-escalate hostilities and restart healthier discussions later.

Either way, maintain your dignity and set compassionate boundaries if others play dirty. You will guide everyone to calmer waters simply by insisting on higher standards.

And with that, I hope you feel much more prepared now to maintain control, influence, and perspective in the hottest spotlight!

Move forward with confidence to skillfully handle any storm. And remember, your inner state of mind determines outer reality - so conduct yourself accordingly!

BARGAINING STRATEGIES: TECHNIQUES TO GET THE BEST DEAL

Now that we've covered the bases of effective negotiation, it's time to dive into more advanced bargaining and closing tactics.

This chapter will provide a robust arsenal of tested strategies for extracting the most favorable terms possible in any deal - without manipulation or underhanded tactics.

Specifically, we will look at:

- Why the most aggressive bargaining style often fails

- How to determine your ideal reserve points and starting goals

- Persuasive techniques to frame value

- Strategic concession tools like "if...then"

- Signals to bid first or second

- Dealing with ultimatums and pressure tactics

- Closing the deal at the right time

Armed with this expansive repertoire, you can confidently navigate any negotiation by obtaining the best possible terms while protecting relationships and reputation.

So let's start by looking at why the wrong approach to bargaining often backfires...

Why a Confrontational Style Fails

First, it is important to understand that there are basically 2 general approaches to bargaining and price negotiations:

- *Confrontational*

- *Collaborative*

confrontational style , each side competes in a battle of wills to "win" and extract the most of the limited value at the table. Aggressive communications and ultimatums are common.

Unfortunately, this approach antagonizes the other party, destroying the trust and goodwill necessary to explore creative win-win solutions.

Furthermore, the other party will likely counterattack with equally harsh tactics, putting the entire future relationship at risk for some short-term gains.

In contrast, the collaborative style involves a joint search for fair terms that benefit both sides. It leverages open-ended questions, creative brainstorming, and mutual compromises to expand the total "pie," not just divide a fixed size.

Of course, sometimes you will need to take firm stances about your needs. But do it without the bravado or rigidity that burns bridges unnecessarily. You can be assertive and flexible at the same time.

Therefore, avoid confrontational weapons such as bluffs, ultimatums, manipulation or veiled threats. Instead, build goodwill and explore expansive win-win options. Your counterpart will be much more willing to work with you in good faith.

Now that we understand the right mindset, let's dive into some specific tactics...

ESTABLISHING YOUR INITIAL AND FINAL LIMITS

Before entering into any serious negotiations, you must have complete clarity on:

- *Your starting position:*

> The ideal starting point from which you will start trading

- *Your final limit:*

> The furthest concession you are willing to make to seal the deal

Your starting position should obviously ask for more than you expect to actually receive. But it must also be realistic enough not to be dismissed out of hand, which undermines its credibility.

Carefully analyze:

- Current average market value

- The best terms other buyers received

- How desperately you need to close this deal

- How much this specific party usually gives up in negotiations

As for your final limit, this is the point beyond which you would simply walk away from the table. Determining this in advance removes emotions from the equation, ensuring you don't make unreasonable concessions in the heat of the moment and later regret it.

Aligning these two anchors provides the boundaries within which you have room to operate.

Next step...how to frame the value of your offer in a compelling way!

FRAMING YOUR VALUE PERSUASIVELY

Master negotiators and salespeople understand the immense power of skillfully framing any proposal in a way that resonates with the other party's deepest interests and values.

Instead of just stating a number, they wrap their offer inside a captivating story backed by solid evidence.

For example, to justify a **PREMIUM price** , emphasize exceptional results that other customers have achieved. Or demonstrate how your product will save much more than its cost over 5 years of use.

Another approach is to tie your value to broader metrics important to the customer like user satisfaction, sustainable innovation, contributions to the community, or centralization of digital security.

Overall, the more meaning and impact you attach to your price, the more persuasive your proposal becomes. People trade based on perceived value, not just absolute numbers.

So wrap each offer in terms that resonate deeply as a compelling story, not just cold statistics.

LEVERAGING STRATEGIC CONCESSION TECHNIQUES

A critical issue in any bargain is how to sequence concessions to extract the best terms without conceding too much too soon.

A skillful technique for doing this is to link each concession to a proportional benefit to the other party. In other words:

"If you do X, then I can do Y"

> For example:

>> "If we can extend the service contract from 1 year to 3 years, then I can reduce the annual fee by 10%."

This allows you to make bigger bargains that benefit your side, attached with enough corresponding benefits to encourage the other party to agree.

This bonding approach also protects against giving too much unilaterally without getting anything in return. You maintain the central balance of power.

> Some additional variations include:

>> "If we can change the delivery date to the 15th, I will increase the discount to 12%."

>> "I can provide 24-hour support if our monthly fee increases by $5 per user to cover costs."

See how by diplomatically linking **DEMANDS** to **CONCESSIONS** you can negotiate much more favorable terms without appearing inflexible or greedy?

SIGNS TO OFFER FIRST OR WAIT

Sometimes presenting the first offer gives you the advantage of anchoring the other party's expectation around your starting number.

But offering first also takes away your valuable power to react, negotiate, and bargain from there.

So what's the best move?

Well, it entirely depends on whether you are trading in a buyer's or seller's market.

In **BUYER markets** where there is a lot of demand and little supply, sellers often need to quote first. But in seller's markets, buyers often wait for the seller to set expectations.

In addition to the market environment, your relative power of influence and the urgency of the parties also affect who should go first.

But regardless of who makes the first offer, you now have powerful tools to respond strategically from there, making it the floor, not the final ceiling!

RESPONDING TO ULTIMATES AND OTHER PRESSURE TACTICS

Occasionally during a negotiation, the other party may try to force you to make concessions through bluffs, false ultimatums, or other manipulative tricks.

Never rush or stop in despair when this happens! Instead, respond calmly by stating your absolute terms or conditions clearly.

> For example:

>> "I cannot agree to such a tight timeline given the substantial scope. The earliest we could deliver a responsible solution would be in 10 weeks."

> Or if you really don't need the deal that much, you can just politely call the bluff :

>> "If this deadline cannot be extended, I completely understand if you need to look for another option. I wish you the best."

This rarely fails to cause the other party to backtrack on the unreasonable demand. But if they don't back down, you should also be prepared to walk away from the deal, keeping your dignity intact.

In general, when faced with pressure tactics, remain firm on principles while flexible on details. This protects you while still demonstrating reasonableness.

Recognizing the right time to close

Knowing exactly **WHEN** to close the deal is also essential to ensure you don't leave money on the table prematurely.

So how do you know when the time is right?

Here are the main signs:

- When you have achieved most of your major non-negotiable goals

- When multiple rounds of bargaining have already occurred without significant new gains

- When you have exhausted other levers or bargaining chips in the conversation

- When final satisfaction questions are answered positively

In other words, keep trading until moving further puts already secured gains at risk without enough extra commensurate potential.

At the point where you've achieved the major victory while protecting the relationship and goodwill, extending much beyond that often produces diminishing marginal gains.

It's better to consolidate and protect what you've already achieved - and then rely on additional future negotiations for further incremental improvements. Your counterpart will be much more open once a fair deal has been reached and the dust has settled.

IDENTIFYING AND USING 'BLACK SWANS': REVEALING AND EXPLORING HIDDEN INFORMATION

This chapter will cover a powerful concept that can make a big difference to your negotiation skills: "black swans."

What are black swans? They are unlikely, high-impact and difficult to predict events. In other words, they are surprises that have significant consequences. They often reveal valuable information that was previously hidden or not considered.

In negotiation, identifying potential black swans can give you a crucial advantage. You can anticipate scenarios that others don't see and be prepared to exploit them to your advantage. This chapter will explain how to do this.

First, we'll talk about how black swans relate to negotiation. Then we'll look at how to identify them more efficiently and explore the information they reveal. Finally, I will present some ways to incorporate this approach into your trading strategies.

If applied correctly, the black swan concept can greatly improve your results. So let's dive into this topic!

THE IMPACT OF BLACK SWANS ON NEGOTIATION

The "black swans" metaphor was popularized by writer and former Wall Street trader Nassim Nicholas Taleb . In his 2007 bestseller, "The Logic of the Black Swan," Taleb argues that major historical events and scientific advances are often unpredictable results of unlikely causes.

These events have three main characteristics:

- They are unlikely and difficult to predict with traditional methods.

- They have an extreme and far-reaching impact.

- Even after they occur, they still seem unlikely and unpredictable. We can only rationalize them retroactively.

Famous examples include the rise of the internet, the 9/11 attacks, and the 2008 global financial crisis.

In individual negotiations, black swans can come in two main forms:

- Unforeseen changes in the context: new external events that completely alter the scenario, opening up new possibilities and closing others. For example: an economic crisis, a competitor that is left out of the market, a new disruptive technology.

- New information about the other party: you discover something unexpected and important about whoever is negotiating with you. This completely changes your view and strategy on that specific negotiation.

Identifying potential black swans is crucial to preparing for the unexpected and exploiting it to your advantage.

Skilled negotiators are always vigilant, looking for signs of unforeseen changes in context or hidden information about the other party. This way, they can adapt quickly and take advantage of these surprises.

Now let's look at some ways to reveal and exploit these "black swans" in your negotiations.

IDENTIFYING BLACK SWANS MORE EFFICIENTLY

There are certain principles and techniques that can increase your chances of spotting black swans earlier than others. Here are some tips for keeping an eye out for these surprise events:

- Question standard assumptions and expectations

    A black swan often seems impossible precisely because we make unconscious assumptions about what "should" happen. For example, assuming that an important customer will always meet contract deadlines. Or that a certain competitor will not enter our region of operation. Challenge these assumptions by analyzing alternatives and less likely scenarios. This will broaden your vision.

- Study exceptions and anomalies

Pay close attention to data that "doesn't fit." Atypical cases can signal broader changes in the future. For example, a regional customer begins placing orders well above normal, perhaps indicating expansion into other areas.

- Hear perspectives from outside the bubble

Seek diverse opinions, especially from people outside your immediate circle. They can notice patterns that you don't see. Talk to customers, partners, operational-level employees, people from other industries.

- Analyze micro signals

Pay attention to the slightest signs, such as subtle changes in the other party's tone of voice or body language, words that are different from usual, hesitations, etc. Detecting these signals helps identify hidden information.

- Use simulations and visualizations

Carry out hypothetical exercises, simulating alternative and unlikely scenarios. Or visualize, vividly and in detail, how these situations would play out and how you would act. This expands your ability to recognize and leverage black swans.

These are just a few ways to increase your "sensitivity" to unexpected events and information. The more you practice, the better you will get.

Now let's look at what to do when a black swan actually appears.

EXPLORING HIDDEN INFORMATION REVEALED BY BLACK SWANS

Detecting a black swan in time is already a big step. But the best thing about them is that these events often reveal valuable information previously hidden or unnoticed.

Whether it is a drastic change in the external context or new information about the other party, the black swan signals a break from what was expected. This opens up space for new possibilities and creative approaches.

In a negotiation, when a black swan arises, you must respond quickly and assertively, exploring its implications to the fullest:

- Investigate the new situation in depth

Ask lots of questions to understand exactly what has changed, why and how it affects trading.

- Evaluate previously unfeasible options

What does this new scenario allow or exclude in terms of possible agreements? Which approaches make the most sense now?

- Identify levers and weaknesses

Where is the other party most vulnerable with this game changer? And where are you? Adapting the strategy to explore these points is key.

- Modify demands and offers

Adjust your terms, prices, conditions, etc., to make them compatible with the new reality and get the most out of it.

- Communicate strategically

Use incisive communication, focused on what this revealed information changes in the negotiation and the relationship. This increases your chances of a much better deal.

It is also worth highlighting that sometimes the black swan completely changes the view you had about that other party. Maybe they're not exactly who you imagined. Or your real interests are quite different from what they seemed before.

At these times, it is essential to suspend previous judgments and put aside first impressions. Focus only on what matters now: deeply understanding this new perspective and exploring it in the best way possible.

Now that we've seen the main concepts, it's time for the most important part: how to apply this in real life.

INTEGRATING BLACK SWANS INTO YOUR TRADING STRATEGIES

There are several ways to put this mentality of identifying and harnessing black swans into practice. Here are some tips for incorporating this into your daily life:

Before negotiations:

Analyze the context broadly, questioning limiting assumptions about what can or cannot suddenly change.

Research a lot about all parties involved, seeking to deeply understand their business models, strategic priorities, typical approaches, etc. This helps you notice contradictory information that may arise later.

Visualize alternatives, imagining context changes and new revelations that would alter your strategy. This lessens the surprise factor if these situations actually happen.

During negotiations:

Listen very carefully to everything others say, especially signs that contradict previous assumptions about them.

Ask "what if…" questions, exploring options and information that no one has considered. This could reveal potential black swans.

Meticulously observe body language and other micro-signals, picking up any hint of nonverbal changes in others' posture.

When a surprise arises, investigate it further by asking direct, incisive questions. Don't be afraid to face new information head-on, no matter how shocking it may be.

After negotiations:

Revisit processes, analyzing where your initial assumptions failed and what contradictory information or changes in context were decisive.

Consider improvements to your research and preparedness systems to close gaps that prevented early detection of these surprises.

There are many other ways to apply the black swan mentality. The main thing is to always keep it in mind, expect the unexpected and prepare to explore new situations to your advantage.

In this chapter, you saw a new model for approaching negotiations: considering the possibility of black swans, unlikely but impactful events that reveal valuable hidden information.

We have seen the main characteristics of these surprise events and how they can arise in negotiations. Then, we look at ways to identify them more efficiently and make the most of the new perspectives they bring.

Finally, you've received several practical tips on how to integrate this mindset into your future trade preparation, execution, and review.

Mastering this topic can completely change your results, allowing you to anticipate and take advantage of information that others don't see. You are able to masterfully explore even the most unpredictable scenarios!

In the next chapter, we'll dive into another essential concept: ensuring the execution of agreements. See how to ensure that what was agreed will actually happen in practice.

ENSURING EXECUTION: HOW TO ENSURE AGREEMENTS ARE COMPLIED WITH

In the previous chapter, we talked about how to identify and explore "black swans"—unlikely events that reveal valuable hidden information. Using this mindset will greatly improve your ability to deal with surprises and unpredictable scenarios.

Now, we will dive into another crucial concept: ensuring the execution of closed agreements. After all, there is no point in being an excellent negotiator and closing great deals if they are not fulfilled later!

This will be a chapter for you to really master this topic. We'll see:

- Why ensuring execution is essential

- The 5 steps to business that will come to fruition

- Legislative and enforcement techniques

- Adapting monitoring to the context

- Dealing with unforeseen events in execution

- Closing the gaps that allowed non-compliance

By the end of this chapter, you will be able to make solid agreements that will be effectively delivered by all parties. Let's start!

WHY GUARANTEING EXECUTION IS ESSENTIAL

In many negotiations, closing the deal already seems like an excellent outcome. We made concessions, aligned terms, overcame impasses. It seems that the hardest part is behind us.

However, in fact, the biggest challenge is often precisely ensuring that everything agreed is actually delivered afterwards! Statistics show that more than 70% of business agreements are not fully executed.

This happens for several reasons: changes in the scenario, communication failures, priorities that change over time, etc. But largely, the problem lies in the way the original negotiation was conducted. We have not created mechanisms strong enough to guarantee execution over time. It is only based on trust or fragile promises.

This is why experienced negotiators invest so much time in eliminating uncertainty about future delivery. They know that the agreement will only have real value if it becomes a complete reality. Otherwise, all efforts will have been in vain.

Ensuring execution should be one of your top priorities when negotiating. In the next section, we will look at a structured roadmap to achieve this goal.

THE 5 BUSINESS STEPS THAT WILL COME TO THE FORE

There is a well-defined process used by high-level negotiators to make their agreements a reality:

Step 1: Eliminate ambiguities

First, maximum clarity is needed about exactly what each side promises to deliver, and when. Everything must be extremely well defined, with no room for dubious interpretations later.

This involves describing in detail the scope, schedule, milestones, responsible parties, financial terms and all objective metrics of the agreement. Every detail must be crystal clear for both sides.

Step 2: Strengthen Obligations

After eliminating ambiguities, it is time to "toughen" the agreement, creating true obligations that will be fulfilled at all costs by the parties:

Establish very clear expected results, and the consequences if they are not achieved.

Insert financial incentives and penalties associated with compliance (or not) with each milestone into the agreement.

Obtain solid guarantees: guarantors, insurance, bonds. External entities that take responsibility if something goes wrong.

Step 3: Align internal expectations

Often the obstacle lies in the internal execution of each side, not in the relationship between them. Therefore, it is necessary to ensure total alignment within the respective organizations:

Define who are internally responsible in each company to enable this delivery.

Communicate the agreement very clearly to those involved, ensuring that there will be no interpretation noise.

Formally collect acceptance in all areas of the negotiated terms, avoiding surprises.

Step 4: Create follow-up mechanisms

Having done all this, it is still essential to create ways to continuously monitor the progress of the execution:

Establish mandatory periodic communications to check status.

Standardize reporting models or measurement instruments for agreed indicators.

Schedule meetings or conference calls at critical milestones to jointly validate results.

Step 5: Plan quick responses

Even with all this, unforeseen events happen. So, it is crucial to map out in advance how to quickly deal with possible problems:

Create protocols for quickly resolving issues and how to alert about delays or demand adjustments.

Define those responsible for making emergency decisions in each company, if the main ones cannot be contacted.

Establish alternative options if any element of the agreement cannot be fulfilled as originally planned due to sudden changes in the scenario.

This is the ideal flow. Now, let's delve deeper into some key techniques within each step.

LEGISLATIVE AND ENFORCEMENT TECHNIQUES

Within a well-done business agreement, there will always be two complementary layers:

- Legislative clauses: which clearly define the terms themselves, eliminating ambiguities.

- Enforcement mechanisms: which will effectively ensure that everything is fulfilled in practice.

Let's see in more detail how to deal with each one:

Legislative Techniques

These are the provisions of the agreement that describe in crystal clear terms what was agreed between the parties. They make clear, in objective language, all essential metrics and milestones.

Remember: nothing can be implied! Each important element must appear explicitly in the text of the agreement.

Some examples of powerful legislative clauses:

- Detail step by step the scope delivered by each party in each phase.

- Set strict deadlines and dates for achieving specific milestones of the project or contracted service.

- Establish very specific amounts and payment methods, linked to the completion of each stage.

- List financial or operational penalties to be applied in the event of delays or problems in execution.

These items eliminate room for misinterpretation or accidental non-compliance. Everything that will be done is there, black and white, without gaps.

Executory techniques

In turn, enforcement mechanisms aim to ensure that legislative terms will necessarily be complied with. They create consequences and incentives so that everything happens as agreed.

Examples:

- Insurance or financial guarantees provided by third parties that will fully cover the customer if the other party fails to deliver.

- Clauses that provide for the definitive transfer of certain rights, properties or values in the event of non-compliance with the metrics and deadlines defined in the contract.

- Fines or compulsory compensation to be paid automatically if any milestone is not met.

These measures create an environment where it is simply not optional to not comply with the terms. They also facilitate quick resolution or compensation, should something still go wrong.

Ultimately, by combining powerful legislative and enforcement techniques, your agreements will become virtually foolproof during execution.

But not everything is resolved in the text of the contract. The next phase is to create adequate governance structures and monitoring of deliveries.

ADAPTING MONITORING TO THE CONTEXT

In addition to building an armored agreement, it is also crucial to set up intelligent execution monitoring mechanisms. They enable you to quickly detect any problems and take action to resolve them.

However, each negotiation has unique characteristics. Monitoring mechanisms must be adapted case by case, considering:

> **- Size of the agreement:** agreement worth millions of reais justifies more robust structures than smaller deals.

> **- Duration of execution:** deliveries that take months require more structured processes than quick projects.

- **Number of people involved:** more people on both sides increases the risk of noise and requires regular communications.

- **Degree of interdependence:** projects with many continuous integrations between those involved require intensive coordination.

- **Context dynamism:** rapidly changing external scenarios require more frequent checking of assumptions.

- **Size of the risks:** potential catastrophic consequences require heavier preventive efforts.

- **History between the parties:** long-lasting and stable relationships require less supervision than a first joint project.

Calibrate your governance and monitoring mechanisms considering all these elements. Some examples of useful tools:

- Reports or dashboards to track key performance indicators related to milestones.

- Joint committee with leaders from both sides to oversee progress on critical milestones.

- Special audits or quick health assessments when key metrics deviate too far from plan.

The secret is to have instruments that immediately detect any risk to the agreement and allow for corrective actions and measures.

We talk a lot about prevention. But what about when unforeseen events happen anyway?

DEALING WITH UNEXPECTED INCIDENTS IN EXECUTION

No matter how good your preventative techniques are, problems may arise during the execution of the agreement:

> - Context changes that make certain originally agreed terms unfeasible.

> - Misunderstandings or misalignment within one of the parties.

> - Unintentional errors that impact deadlines or deliveries.

> - New leaders who question commitments made previously.

The key is to have mechanisms defined in advance to quickly and objectively resolve any problem. This prevents specific issues from putting the entire agreement at risk.

Some effective protocols for managing unforeseen events:

- **Escalation committee:** forum with executives authorized to make emergency decisions if the original people cannot be consulted in time.

- **Dispute and resolution process:** clearly mapped path to resolve technical or legal disputes quickly, without breaking the agreement.

- **Force majeure clauses:** which remove sanctions if a party absolutely proves that they were not to blame for the problem that arose.

- **External mediators registered in the contract:** consultants or independent companies that help when more serious impasses occur, without the need to go to court.

- **Alternative options or plans B:** secondary paths previously made viable to carry out the same delivery in a different way, if plan A becomes unfeasible for some exceptional reason.

Again, the focus is on ensuring ways to overcome unforeseen events without the agreement itself being affected. This keeps the relationship intact.

Finally, even if all protocols have been followed, a failure can still occur. And now, what to do?

CLOSING THE GAPS THAT ALLOWED NONCOMPLIANCE

After a serious problem in execution, in addition to resolving that specific situation, it is also essential to improve your own processes so that similar failures do not occur again in the future.
It is important to conduct an in-depth analysis, without the intention of finding blame, but learning critical lessons. Ask yourself honestly:

> - What early signs of risk did we miss? How could we have identified them earlier?

> - What clauses or enforcement mechanisms failed to prevent or contain the problem? What could have been done differently?

> - Were our governance protocols and response to unforeseen events not sufficient? What would need to be changed?

> - Are there ambiguities, loopholes or inconsistencies in the original contract that ended up being exploited opportunistically by either side? Where could our writing have been smarter and more foolproof?

Carry out a constructive analysis, focusing on continuous improvement. This will not only make this deal repairable, but it will ensure that you will negotiate and operate much better in the future.

In this chapter, you have seen how vital it is to ensure that agreements are fully executed in practice, and not just on paper.

We look at a 5-step roadmap to maximize those chances, closing loopholes from initial drafting to diligent post-signing follow-up.

You also received several examples of legislative and enforcement techniques to make your contracts much more solid and unforeseen.

Finally, we saw the importance of learning from problems, making continuous improvements in your negotiation processes and operationalization of complex agreements.

I hope this chapter helps you achieve not just temporary victories at the negotiating table, but practical and lasting gains by ensuring the effective implementation of the agreement.

In the next module, we will begin our conclusion by analyzing the path to applying all the content of the book in practice. Until then!

CONCLUSION AND MAP TO ORGANIZE THE SALES AND AFTER-SALES PROCESS IN PRACTICE

We have reached the conclusion of this book on mastery in complex negotiations. More specifically, about how to maximize results by applying advanced concepts.

In the previous pages, we saw two powerful modules:

> - Identifying and exploring black swans: unlikely surprises that open space for new creative approaches.

> - Techniques to guarantee the execution of closed agreements, ensuring that they actually get off the ground.

Now, in this final chapter, I will give an overview of how to balance these views and apply them to masterfully organize your complete consultative sales process and highly complex project management.

I will address this topic in two phases:

> - High-value consultative sales

> - Complex after-sales deliveries

Let's look at best practices in each case.

HIGH-VALUE CONSULTATIVE SALES

You must already be used to traditional sales processes: understanding needs, presenting solutions, showing cases, making proposals, etc.

However, very complex sales require more. You need to go further, conducting truly consultative work with your clients.

This involves working very closely with their senior leadership, practically being a strategic partner. Fundamental differences in this model:

- Focus on business value, more than on proposals and prices: understanding the client's general context and challenges and proposing ways to boost their results.

- Vision for projects and complete deliveries: designing solutions that combine your products/services with changes in processes, operating models and even their organizational culture.

- Contracts linked to strategic customer metrics: your earnings will be linked to the earnings you will generate within critical KPIs: profitability, market share, NPS, etc.

In other words, you will act as a specialist who not only sells, but structures and leads large-scale projects within these organizations.

This requires preparation and sophisticated methodologies in conducting sales. Let's look at some key points .

DEEP RESEARCH AND PLANNING

Before even your first contact with the prospect's senior leadership, your team should dive into extensive research, modeling your context, market and indicators.

It is necessary to go beyond the obvious and bring to light insights that even they were not clear about, exploring unusual connections that you could leverage.

By having a broad and in-depth view of their territory, you can begin to outline alternative paths to generate untapped value.

Only then start your conversations. Demonstrating clear expertise in their real world of activity – at a level that is often more sophisticated than that of the client itself – will be your first major competitive differentiator.

APPROACH THROUGH DEEP PAIN, NOT SURFACE

When talking to business leaders, avoid the trap of focusing on the most obvious and frequent challenges they face. Everyone has tried to solve their superficial problems, without definitive success.

Your goal is to identify much deeper pain, which is at the root and is the real cause of the repetitive symptoms that they have already learned to live with.

This may involve deep-rooted cultural dilemmas, contradictions in internal incentives, historical political conflicts within the organization, etc.

Again, your 360°, multidisciplinary and bias-free view of that environment will allow you to see far beyond generic complaints. By doing this, you will position yourself at the forefront, bringing an approach and level of partnership that no one has presented before.

CONNECTING FINANCIAL RESULTS AND CULTURAL IMPACT

Based on this deep pain identified in your diagnoses, begin to outline a customized solution that combines your products/services with broad changes to processes, organizational structure and internal customer behaviors.

The crucial thing here is to make this integrated proposal very tangible and pragmatic from the beginning. Show exactly how each initiative will influence core financial metrics, while also generating cultural repercussions on the teams' long-term performance.

This mix between immediate gains and lasting behavioral transformations is very powerful and difficult for competitors to copy.

BUILDING THE JUSTIFICATION FOR INVESTMENT

With your proposal already well conceptualized and detailed, it's time to quantify everything into a solid projection of returns.

This justification for the investment must derive very specific values about how much that customized project can add in terms of additional revenue, reduced internal costs, productivity gains, reduced churn , etc. for the client's business in the coming years.

All your numbers must be based on benchmarks, real cases and solid market references. But the final set needs to be specific to that client's unique reality.

Also make conservative, realistic and even pessimistic projections, proving the strength of your model even considering stress scenarios. This way, additional earning opportunities will be seen as a bonus if the real scenario is more positive.

DELIVERING IMPROVEMENTS FROM DAY ONE

A common pitfall in long-term projects is the time needed to generate results that are actually perceived by the client. To avoid anxiety and premature abandonment, you need to ensure quick and relevant wins.

Create automated improvements that can be implemented very early, even before formal approval of the complete project, already bringing visible practical results.

This generates credibility and repeat use, in addition to financing other costs. Don't be afraid to apply your knowledge to improve their internal processes in the first few months.

CONTRACTS LINKED TO SOLID METRIFICATION

We reach another fundamental point: how to link their deliveries and earnings to the strategic KPIs that really matter to their business: regional market share, NPS by buyer segment, etc.

Create a fluid model in which you assume a considerable portion of the risk, with variable gains tied to the measurable success provided within their own critical objectives.

This fully aligns incentives between you, eliminates internal political friction there and shields your projects even when there is a change in leadership. After all, you will only be successful if you effectively deliver what is vital to their strategic perpetuity.

This form of consultative approach, focused on business value and with flexible contracts linked to real gains, is what will make your complex proposals stand out from the competition.

Now, let's talk about the next challenge: ensuring impeccable after-sales deliveries.

COMPLEX AFTER-SALES DELIVERIES

Congratulations! By following the principles above, you must have managed to close several challenging projects with large clients. However, the bigger work starts now.

It's time to execute everything you proposed – and the risks are enormous. A single failure is enough to put your earned reputation at risk. How to proceed?

Below, I'll share a set of best practices to ensure you maximize success on these long journeys full of variables beyond your control.

MAPPING RISKS IN DEPTH

Right after the final contract signing, bring together your internal teams and some client executives for an extensive risk assessment.

The objective is to map absolutely everything that could go wrong in a project of that complexity and with those unique characteristics.

Don't limit yourself to obvious risks. Explore very unusual vulnerabilities, but which may materialize. Analyze interdependencies between systems, areas and business units.

Understand the political dynamics and cultural history behind potential organizational conflicts. Identify potential black swans.

Catalog all threats by crossing impacts and probabilities. And start designing solid contingencies for each of them, avoiding unpleasant surprises later.

FORMALIZATION SUPPORTED BY FLEXIBLE BUSINESS PROCESS MANAGEMENT

With so many internal and external clients involved, your project can quickly get out of hand with misunderstandings or informal communication errors.

Therefore, formalizing absolutely everything in clear business process management is essential. However, these processes cannot be too rigid.

Design well-defined flows, but with conditional algorithms that automatically trigger actions or alerts in the event of deviations or exceptional cases.

This protects execution through formality, but allows adaptability in unusual cases. Invest heavily in process analysts and automation architects to make this possible.

HIGH-LEVEL GOVERNANCE COMMITTEE

Even with everything thoroughly mapped out and processes formalized, an additional layer of oversight is necessary in multifunctional projects: a high-level governance committee.

Bring together periodically (initial monthly rhythm, decreasing according to maturity) the main executives from both sides to check the "pulse" of the project.

Evaluate the formal indicators, but also give space to air out concerns, specific noises not yet addressed by standard structures, etc.

This more political and less technical layer is important to calibrate expectations, align versions and avoid leadership vacuums even with so many people involved.

PREVENTIVE AND CORRECTIVE AUDITS

No matter how excellent your planning, reality is always more complex. Unmapped issues will emerge.

Don't wait for formal performance indicators to take too much away from the goal for you to take action. Pay attention to weak signals: small inconsistencies, localized delays, political cracks , etc.

As soon as something is out of standard, even on a limited scale, trigger a preventive audit, with experts from outside that specific flow.

This external view will help reveal previously unnoticed gaps, as well as alert players to diligently focus on excellence.

Do not punish anyone at this stage (except in cases of bad faith), just correct processes. But make it clear that recurring deviations after corrections will have consequences. This encourages compliance without generating internal fears.

CONTINUOUS MONITORING OF RESULTS

Finally, establish a robust, multifaceted routine for tracking results and formal KPIs throughout all phases.

Use your data analysis to create automatic dashboards, connecting different inputs. Break everything down into specific goals and metrics, units, team, roles, etc.

Value internal transparency, allowing everyone to monitor everyone's performance. This encourages collaboration and quick mutual corrections.

And toast your successes, even incremental ones. Keeping everyone engaged is crucial when you still have a long way to go.

By following these best practices for diligent management of complex projects, your after-sales results will certainly be on par with the excellence already achieved in your high-value-added consultative sales that we know how to do so well!

But this book doesn't end here...

NEXT STEPS

Dear reader, our time together on this book now comes to an end. I hope you were able to absorb the best advanced trading techniques and strategies.

More specifically, how to integrate concepts of identifying hidden opportunities and ensuring execution to enhance your results in multifunctional corporate environments full of complex variables.

However, our work does not stop here. I constantly produce new complementary materials in text, audio and video to further deepen these concepts and show practical applications.

Therefore, if you are not already on our contact list, sign up to receive everything that will be produced from now on. These will be exclusive insights and cases, shared only with our subscriber base.

I hope to meet you again soon to continue this journey of improving your negotiation and sales skills.

As we turn the final page of this journey together, I sincerely hope that the learnings shared here have touched your heart and sparked new perspectives. If this book has brought you any value, I kindly ask that you take a few moments to leave a review on Amazon. Your words not only help me grow and hone my craft, but they also guide other readers in their quests for knowledge and inspiration. Your opinion is a valuable gift, both for me and for the community of readers looking for stories that transform. I sincerely thank you for sharing this journey with me and I hope we can meet again in the pages of a new adventure.

REGINALDO OSNILDO

Hello, I'm Reginaldo Osnildo, author and innovator in the areas of sales, technology, and communication strategies. My experience ranges from the academic environment, as a professor and researcher at the University of Southern Santa Catarina, to practice as a strategist at Grupo Catarinense de Rádios. With a PhD in sales narratives and digital convergence, and a master's degree in storytelling and social imaginary, I bring my readers a unique fusion of theory and practice. My goal is to provide knowledge in a simple, practical and didactic language, encouraging direct application in personal and professional life.

Yours sincerely

Reginaldo Osnildo